T0112389

Angela Porter's

TROPICAL RAINFOREST

HIDDEN PICTURES

Copyright © 2017 by Angela Porter

All rights reserved. No part of this book may be reproduced in any manner without the express written consent of the publisher, except in the case of brief excerpts in critical reviews or articles. All inquiries should be addressed to Racehorse for Young Readers, 307 West 36th Street, 11th Floor, New York, NY 10018.

Racehorse for Young Readers books may be purchased in bulk at special discounts for sales promotion, corporate gifts, fund-raising, or educational purposes. Special editions can also be created to specifications. For details, contact the Special Sales Department, Skyhorse Publishing, 307 West 36th Street, 11th Floor, New York, NY 10018 or info@skyhorsepublishing.com.

Racehorse for Young Readers™ is a pending trademark of Skyhorse Publishing, Inc.®, a Delaware corporation.

Visit our website at www.skyhorsepublishing.com.

10 9 8 7 6 5 4 3 2 1

Cover and interior artwork by Angela Porter

Print ISBN: 978-1-944686-54-3

Printed in the United States of America

Forever Inspired COLORING BOOK

Angela Porter's

TROPICAL RAINFOREST

HIDDEN PICTURES

ANGELA PORTER

FOR YOUNG READERS

Find these hidden pictures throughout the following illustrations!

Tropical Rainforests

Ladybugs		59
Snails		9
Hearts		150
Stars		108

HIDDEN PICTURE ANSWER KEY

1

2

3

4

5

6

7

8

9

10

11

12

13

14

15

16

17

18

19

20

21

22

23

24

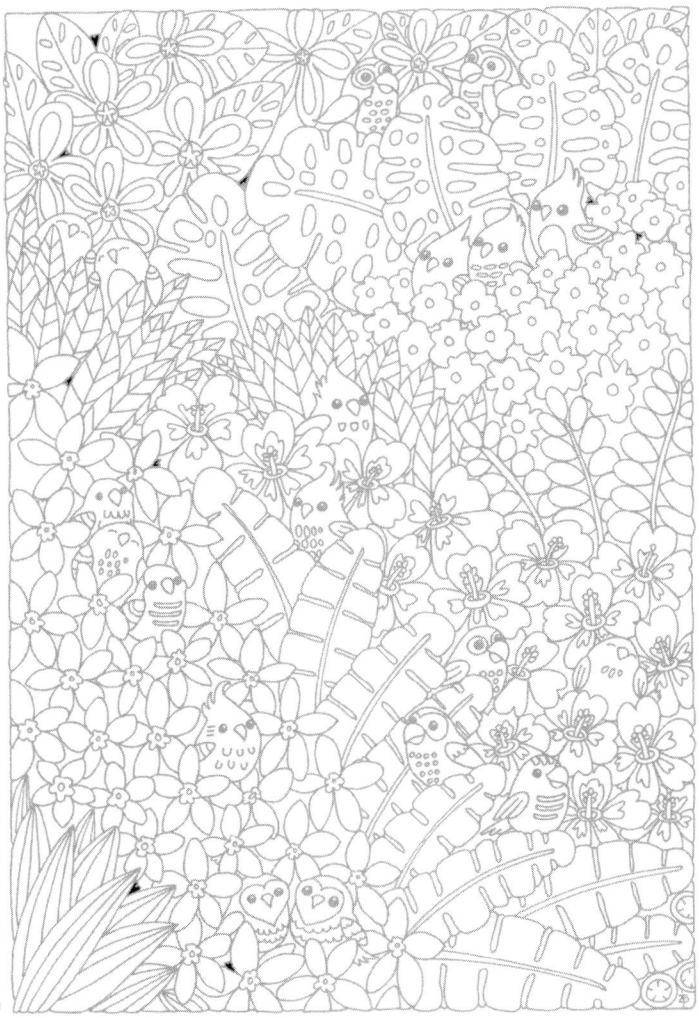

25

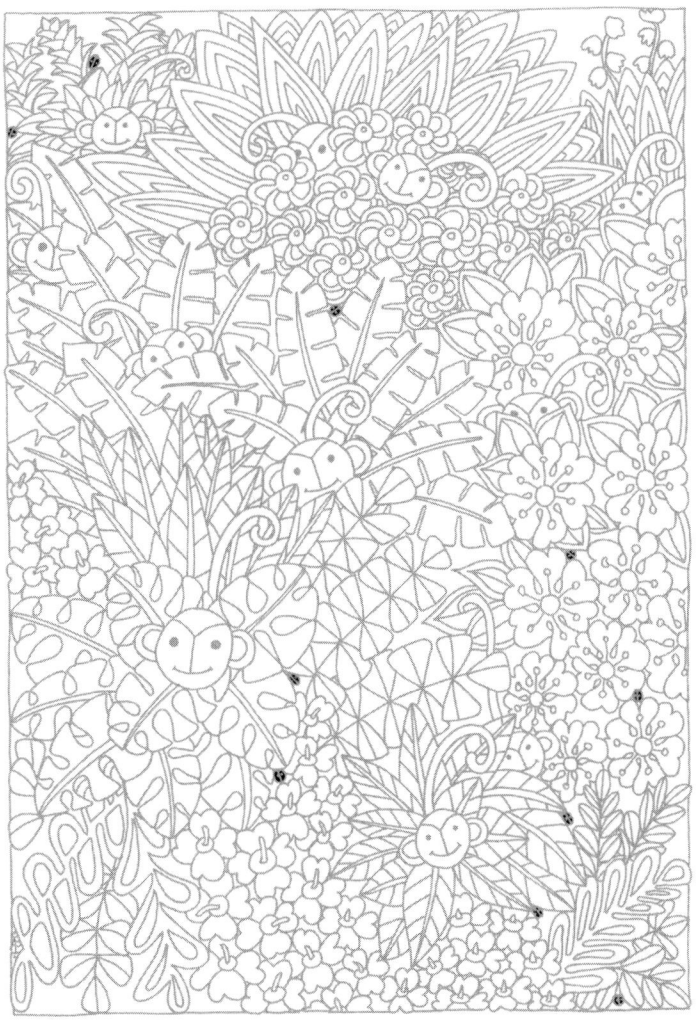

26

27

28

29

30

31

32

33

34

PALETTE BARS

Use these bars to test your coloring medium and palette. Don't be afraid to try unique color combinations!
